M000074167

LOVERS' WEEKEND

LOVERS' WEEKEND

PAUL SCOTT

illustrations by pinglet@pvuk.com

RYLAND
PETERS
& SMALL

LONDON NEW YORK

..ner **Paul Tilby**
..am **Hyslop**
.. **Gavin Bradshaw**
.. **Anne-Marie Bulat**
..ector **Julia Charles**
..Director **Alison Starling**

.. pinglet@pvuk.com

First published in the
United States in 2006
by Ryland Peters & Small, Inc.
519 Broadway
5th Floor
New York, NY 10012
www.rylandpeters.com

10 9 8 7 6 5 4 3 2 1

Text, design, and photographs
© Ryland Peters & Small 2006

ISBN-10: 1 84597 114 0
ISBN-13: 978 1 84597 114 4

Printed in China

CONTENTS

It happens in the strongest of relationships. What began with a seemingly never-ending parade of bouquets, chocolates, and endearments, when the most exciting thing you could both think of doing was having an early night, turns eventually into vegging in front of the TV and quickie sex snatched from the sleeping hours as an afterthought to a hard day, as if it's another thing to check off the to-do list.

Far from what you may think, you don't have to be fed up or regretting your life decisions for your sex life to become a little repetitive.

INTRODUCTION

Successful couples need to be a good team to cope with the demands of modern life. In the course of juggling bills, stress, children, and work, it's perfectly possible for even the happiest couples to find they're seeing less of each other than of the other people they have to deal with. This can put distance between even the most committed partners, who are left wondering if they're still with the same person they met.

Don't let time put out the fire that was lit then. Quite apart from being fun, tending the sexual flame is crucial in keeping a relationship healthy and fresh.

Let this book remind you to set aside time for your partner. By itself, simply remembering that this is a priority will bring you halfway to achieving your amorous aims!

The other half perhaps depends upon imagination. Besides the suggestions in this book, remember your partner's likes and dislikes, and what makes them laugh, too. Reminisce with them about your past sexual experiences together. See if their favorite times differ from yours, and why. Reach back and pick out all the things that made your romance exciting, fun, and unpredictable. And go ahead and keep your partner on their toes, too. Have fun reminding yourselves why you got together to begin with!

SETTING THE SCENE

Take a fresh look at your home. It's easy to forget that your sex life needs a haven in which it can blossom. When it comes to intimacy, does your environment work against you? Even if it's clean and cheerful, it perhaps may not be much of a space in which you'd seduce or be seduced. Sure, experiment a bit. You may want to make love in as many places—in both your home and the world—as you can! But to sustain a course of intimacy with your partner means that your pleasures must have a "home;" somewhere you both can think of as a private space in which to relax, away from the cares of the world.

To that end, endeavor not to let the worldly cares encroach on your bedroom—set up desks, computers, piles of work, and bills elsewhere in your home. Is your furniture comfortable, flexible? Does its feng shui suit seamless seduction? Does the arrangement of furniture and ornaments lead you naturally to the places where you can relax? And busy people can be forgiven for leaving clutter, but nothing will detract more quickly from a smoothly developing session of lovemaking, or burst the bubble of your post-coital mood, than a stubbed toe or a painful stumble for you or your lover.

CREATING A HAVEN

It's simple to transform your home into an environment conducive to love and romance.

Smell is the sense that most triggers our memory, and yet it's easily forgotten, so avoid becoming associated with dank and fusty smells by keeping your home aired and perfumed. Flowers fill a room with life and a sense of abundance, as well as smelling good.

Make sure your bedroom is warm enough that you can be comfortably naked in it. Whether it's condoms, a kinky toy or two, or something to drink, make sure that you have everything at hand that you may want to use to enhance your lovemaking, so that neither of you then has to venture into the cold.

Lastly, give thought to some lighting: both low-watt bulbs and down-lighting flatter (make them as operable as possible from the bed). Making the room more inviting will give you both an incentive to spend more time there.

RELAX & UNWIND

Along with the bullish advice we receive from lifestyle magazines on how to improve our stamina and technique, remember that sexual satisfaction lies chiefly in being able to relax with your partner to begin with. Making your bodies feel great will make your minds receptive to the possibility of their feeling even better when you finally make love!

Not feeling under pressure to have great sex is the first step in making it happen. You're not obliged to have sex and, if you're going to, it should be because you want to, not feel you have to. So if you have resentments between you, work them out rather than putting them to one side, if possible. Be true to yourselves. Take a walk in a beautiful place together, or share a romantic meal. Make room to open up to each other first—allow space for arousal to happen.

You might wish to try: a warm bath, together or alone; aromatherapy herbs for the bathroom or bedroom can really work, leaving one inexplicably lifted and happy; or else reconnect with your lover's body through a sensual massage, relieving stress and tension and lessening the impact of worries on their mind.

✱ *You can never have too many pillows and cushions, either for relaxing or supporting your bodies. Keep plenty around your bed, and simply toss them aside if they're in the way.*

✱ *Candles are a cliché for good reason. The right lighting is essential. Downlighting or shaded lighting is better than harsh overhead light every time.*

✱ *Treat your partner to a bath. The simple act of running or drawing it for them is easily achieved, and yet a clear signal that you want them to relax.*

✱*Pamper one another and see where it leads.*

TIPS

✱ *Provided they aren't allergic, flowers—especially colorful, large, and fragrant ones—are bound to provide your partner with a frisson of romance. Don't leave them in the vase; sprinkle them in the bathtub, too.*

✱ *Don't forget the power of mother nature. A breathtaking mountain top, a sunset at the beach, cool, running water... natural wonders are the most romantic there are. But don't forget a blanket—cold will soon bring you back down to earth.*

✱ *It's worth paying for quality bed linens. Are yours soft and welcoming to your skin?*

SEDUCTION

You may not feel like a siren or a stripper and your partner may not feel much like a silver-tongued devil, even when they're hungry like the wolf. If the thought of seducing someone makes you feel more self-conscious than the most wilting of wallflowers, remember that when pushing someone's buttons it's often the thought that really counts.

Talk about your plans and, gently, about what you'd like to have happen. A new partner can't be blamed for not reading your mind, while a long-term partner will love being reminded that you don't want to let them get away! Get their mind going with visions of what you imagine doing to them. If you remember a mind-blowing occasion, talk about it. Stir those feelings you experienced when you were reaching your peak.

Lastly, seduction isn't all about sex! A bit of old-fashioned consideration goes a long way to making someone feel special. Keep an eye on the drinks, etc., and keep in mind any small needs of your partner's. This way, they can relax (without overdoing it, of course, so they feel like they can't ask for themselves).

FLIRTING

Don't be nervous—flirting is one of the most enjoyable parts of dating, and puts the excitement back into long-term relationships, too. Even if we're not aware of it, we all use body language, sending out messages that show we're interested in someone. Being aware of what you are saying with your body is as important as what comes out of your mouth.

• Pinning your arms to your sides sends out a forbidding message, while showing the insides of your wrists signifies approachability. Arms are one of the main areas in which gender differences are visible —soft and feminine, or veined, strong, and manly. Draw attention to your arms with accessories such as bracelets, or with a chunky watch if you're a man.

• Show some leg. We tend to point our feet towards someone we're interested in. Stroking a thigh will suggest to your partner that they could do the same and, if you're a woman, you might dangle your shoe seductively on your toes.

• If a person mirrors your body language, it shows they're interested. Face the person with your torso.

• Women find broad shoulders attractive in men, so men can try sitting with their shoulders back, which also signifies approachability. Meanwhile, women's shoulders are said to remind men of breasts—smooth and round. Bare shoulders will suggest more.

• Playing with your hair mimics how you'd like others to handle you, while hiding behind long hair makes for seductive glances.

• Candlelight and low lighting make the pupils of our eyes dilate, as they do when we're sexually interested. You might want to stare at your date all night, but it's not very arousing. Hold a gaze for a few seconds and break away. Don't linger, and don't focus on one body part—both genders feel uncomfortable with this. Cast an appreciative gaze without staring.

• Mouth-to-mouth. You're using it to chat, and maybe kiss, so the mouth is an object of attention—lips become redder and more swollen when aroused. Licking and moistening your lips can be sexy, so long as it is not overdone.

KISSING

We can be guilty of neglecting kissing if we're in a long-term relationship; when we know a partner's pathways to arousal, we tend to use them first. We may kiss as we go, but it's not the same as necking for a long time, exploring the other person's responses with your kiss, but also treating the kiss as a novelty and an end in itself. Kiss in places other than in the bedroom, and not just as foreplay. Kissing is safe, and it is legal in public. So make a point from time to time of kissing for its own sake.

• Kissing someone's eyes is a gentle, tender, and sometimes surprising favor. Kiss their eyelids gently, with your mouth against the orbit of their eye. In kissing generally, feeling your partner's eyelids flutter, like feeling and tasting their breath, can be a powerfully arousing reminder of your physical closeness.

• Use your fingers to trace the outline of your lover's lips. You can look into each other's eyes as they get used to the rougher texture of fingers and thumbs.

• Gently hold your lover's lower lip between your finger and thumb and roll it, or else take it into your mouth and suck it. The skin of the lower lip gives easily enough for this gesture of pure desire.

• Put your fingers to each other's lips and move them gently in and out of the mouth. It's not surprising that this action is arousing, since it mirrors penetration itself.

• Play with your partner's face as you kiss. Reach up with your fingertips to caress your partner's cheek; take their ears between your thumbs and forefingers, playing gently, and run your hands around the line of their jaw.

• Breathe each other's breath. Make an airtight seal with your lips and inhale deeply.

• Just grazing each other's lips can be intensely arousing—it's an intimate tease. You can also lick and blow on your partner's lips, making their already sensitized surface tingle at the contrast between warm and cool.

• Butterfly kisses are a similarly teasing treat: pepper your partner's face and neck with small, dry kisses from your puckered lips.

• Tickle your partner's palate and gums with your tongue—you'll be saying intimately how much you want them.

MASSAGE

According to holistic theories of medicine, the power of touch can be one of the most genuine healers and stress relievers in the world. Sometimes partners don't give a good massage because they are lazy, but sometimes, too, it's because they are a little shy. Like dancing, if you don't think you're any good then you are less likely to give yourself the chance to improve. No one likes to be a loser. But massage is essentially about loving touch, which is central to being a lover.

You can give your lover a good rub without oils, but, to add a bit of ritual to signal that you're giving a relaxing massage, oils are, well, essential. You need a greasy, slippery skin surface if you want to reach your partner's knotted, tense muscles without causing friction burns to the skin. Oil is great, too, if your lover is hairy or fleshy. Baby oil or cosmetic oils are fine, while your best option is a neutral massage oil—such as almond or peach nut—which can be mixed with essential oils of your choice. Essential oils should never touch the skin undiluted, as they can be powerfully caustic. And, of course, warm any lubrication you use between your hands first.

Alternatively, burn these aromatherapy oils in an oil burner. Good smells have great effects when your lover's relaxed and breathing deeply, and will really give them the impression you know what you're doing. However, avoid these oils altogether if there's even a chance that you or your partner might be pregnant. Otherwise, oils of lavender, eucalyptus, basil, and bergamot, along with rose, sandalwood, neroli (orange blossom), and ylang ylang, are mood enhancers and reputedly aphrodisiac.

Make sure you are clear whether you're giving an arousing, foreplay massage or a truly relaxing experience after which nothing is expected of your lover but to stay in the relaxed space you've created. Few things will be more annoying for both of you than finding you've confused these goals. If you're taking the latter option, remove all mental pressures and, whether with long, gliding strokes or kneading and squeezing ones, let them empty their minds of everything but sensation.

FOOD & APHRODISIACS

Food and intimacy have always gone together, not least because a meal together is one of the few dates or celebratory occasions when—as opposed to being entertained—you can settle down together, talk, and anticipate (perhaps) the lovemaking to come. Anthropologically, food is associated with intimacy since it's believed that kissing developed from the passing of food from one mouth to another.

Take care not to overdo it with rich sauces; stick to high-protein but light foods (Japanese, Chinese, and Thai foods are quickly metabolized and full of energy). Researchers believe that commonly accepted aphrodisiacs such as asparagus and oysters make little difference, but that doesn't mean they're not sensual and fun. Whatever their physical effects, sucking and swallowing some of these salty, spicy, even semen-like tastes can be pretty suggestive. But take care around eyes—the tastier the food, the more it probably stings.

• Licorice, bananas, ginger, fennel, lettuce, and honey are proven aphrodisiacs.

• Little champagne bubbles popping against your skin is a tasty sensation. If you don't drink alcohol, sparkling mineral water will do just fine.

• Experiment with foods and temperatures, but avoid hot food, of course. Room temperature to freezing is variety enough. Perhaps blindfold your partner, and have them guess what the foods and fruits you produce for them are, from their smell, feel, and texture. Ice cream, fancy fruits, and honey all make a delicious feast of sexy fun. Don't stick to sweet foods, either—all the old jokes about cucumbers are true!

That may be a little *9½ Weeks* for you, or else the thought of all that mess in the kitchen might be less than arousing! If so, it's nonetheless worth knowing that including a few of the following regularly in your diet might improve your sex life. Avocados contain potassium and vitamin B6, two elements that help to enhance male and female libido. Almonds help provide the raw material for a man's healthy production of hormones. Meanwhile, their smell is pleasantly arousing, too.

Eggs are high in vitamins B5 and B6, and help to balance hormone levels and fight stress, two things crucial to a healthy libido. If they sound like rather an everyday tip, think of their value as a fertility symbol, or take a jar of caviar to bed with you! Lastly, of course, an honorable mention for chocolate, which contains phenylethylamine, a chemical which produces feelings of being in love, so there is science behind our enduring love of it!

✱ When the situation's right, kiss each other all over. Until you've kissed every inch of your lover's body, you can't be sure exactly what effect it may have. Treat the areas your partner likes you to caress to more lingering attention.

✱ Cook for your partner wearing nothing but your sexiest underwear.

✱ Try hand-feeding each other with erotic fruits and see where it leads.

✱ Have a three-minute kiss.

TIPS

* *Seduction is not a by-numbers ritual. If you've fallen into a pattern, do it in reverse order.*

* *Give your lover a Thai massage. As a novice, you won't help their muscle tone, but you might turn them on. A large bathroom is best. Lying on towels, lather yourselves liberally with soap and water. The person giving the massage supports their own body weight, but rolls their body along their partner's.*

* *Stroke each other's hair while you're kissing.*

FANTASIES

Playing out a "scene" and assuming characters doesn't mean you're not interested in who each other really is—quite the opposite, as your partner may also be getting in touch with parts of themselves they didn't know existed.

Develop as much of a storyline as you like. You might not feel you'll be able to keep a straight face, but then again humor can be an essential safety valve and a saving grace during sex, in which powerful feelings can sometimes come to the fore unexpectedly. If you're both equally keen, then set aside some time to really indulge your fantasies, when worldly worries are least likely to intrude and you won't watch the clock. Plan ahead, thinking carefully through details, plots, and accessories.

Many magazine articles recommend making a date with each other and pretending to be strangers as a way of putting the spark back in your relationship. However, have you ever thought of doing it not as a remedial treatment but as a bit of fun? It's a good starting point for the very act of pretending that things are different from usual.

PRIVATE DANCER

If you really want to make each other's bodies surrender, and to really lose your self-consciousness, you must be able have sex with each other's minds! If you find it hard to be open about your fantasies, then remember you don't have to divulge them all.

Tell him, for example, about the one in which you are a lapdancer in a gentlemen's club, performing your act—described in salacious detail of course—in front of an audience of (mostly) men.

You have no idea who he is but you spot him, smart and relaxed, sitting at a table. Among a gallery of other men, you begin to silently seduce only him. Describe how you would introduce your breasts to his face, and, as you looked into his eyes, shimmy your bottom in his lap until— in a private moment in a public place—you feel his arousal.

Remember that fantasies are not necessarily things you'd really like to have happen—we just inhabit a fantasy space while we're fantasizing. So there's no need to dwell, for example, on the financial hardships which may have led your "character" to lapdancing! It also means there's no need to be ashamed of them. Combine the thrill of exhibitionism with—for him—the flattering thought that his "character" is special and different enough to approach.

COURTLY LOVE

Even though many of us may not have been inclined to listen intently at school, there's no doubt that English literature has always reflected and inspired sexual fantasies.

It started in the 12th century, at the flirtatious court of Eleanor of Aquitaine and Henry II. While crusading knights put their feet up with heroic Norse sagas as if they were Tom Clancy stories, their wives were excited by romantic tales of courtly love, told by seductive troubadours, which were the "chick-lit" of their day.

The knights in these stories weren't short of dragon-slaying power, but when it came to love they were in thrall to their ladies as if they were their "liege lords." The women were on top—often married—and, when the knights couldn't court them, they expressed their love with brave deeds instead.

When it comes to understanding some of the strange, arousing puzzles of human sexuality, we can do a lot worse than curling up with a good book. Try recreating these courtly tales of love with your partner.

FAR & AWAY

Being away from home together is a tonic for any relationship, so why not think about the role-play possibilities a new, temporary environment might afford?

Hotel rooms often have a sense of corporate anonymity that might fuel a paid-for fantasy of businessman and call-girl, while others have a whiff of a sleazy motel, full of possibilities. Or, if you're lucky enough, your suite might make you feel like a duchess and her manservant on a grand tour!

Why not try going through each other's wardrobes. Even if cross-dressing strikes you as something you'd never pull off, why not see what you'd look like in each other's clothes? She might look bold, assertive, or androgynous in one of his suits, while for him the early moments of transformation can be a revelation! The strange feeling of the other sex's clothing will be an insight in itself.

✱ *Harness the power of your imagination when you're making love—for fantasy, sure, but also for empathy. Think about how it might physically feel to have the others sex's genitals, and think about the sensations your actions are causing your lover to have. Imagine what it feels like to receive the strokes you are administering.*

✱ *Take it in turns to do everything you tell each other to do, for an agreed period of time.*

TIPS

* *Dress your partner for sex.*

* *If your lover's bashful about expressing their fantasies, get them to write down something lewd they'd like to do with you. Then get them to read it aloud.*

* *Think of your darkest desire—now.*

* *Tie your partner's hands before you strip seductively for them. You'll be both submissive (exposing yourself to them) and dominant (restraining them).*

GAMES

You can re-energize your lovemaking by getting a little more risqué and playful in the bedroom, whether it involves sexy board games, candles, costumes, uniforms, or any other paraphernalia. Becoming more provocative together will put a fresh spin on a partner you have come to know well. Playing is the first structured way in which we learn about other people, and it's great to discover the quirky, individual, and unselfconscious sides of your lover.

Sure, a sex-game can be a once- or twice-in-a-lifetime experience; an elaborate gift that indulges your partner's deepest fantasies and for which they'll be grateful ever after. It can also be easy and spontaneous to play, however, and to make a regular feature of your love life. There's a host of simple ideas that involve the most harmlessly obvious form of reverse psychology to get what you want! Have you ever instructed your lover to please you without using their hands, for example, or using *only* their hands? Have you ever suggested they ignore parts of your body and focus on others alone? Making a game of sex may not be just a way of getting what you want, either, but of finding out what else you like! When it comes to giving each other a few surprises, games are the way to go.

PRIVATE INVESTIGATIONS

The following game provides a structure for getting to know each other's responses a little better.

One of you takes charge, perhaps after an evening out, or an event you have shared together. Set the scene, complete with candles and some mellow, sexy music. Ask your lover to strip slowly and watch them, letting your gaze linger appreciatively on each area of flesh that's revealed. The exhibitionist in them will find this really hot.

Strip off, too, if it makes them feel at ease, or else they might get a kick out of you being clothed and dominant while they are naked and vulnerable. When they are naked, have them lie down. Now it's time for you to undertake the most thorough investigation of their pleasure centers they've ever had.

Start with your partner's neck, face, and ears, taking in every nook and cranny with your tongue, lips, and fingertips. Give them a pleasure scale of one to five. Ask them to score how much pleasure they are getting from each place. Ask as you nibble and caress, "Do you like having your neck bitten, like this?" "Do you like having your breasts licked...like this?"

Work your way down your lover's body, from their temples to their toes and back again, and don't miss a spot. Making a point of learning how to please your partner will impress them no end, and could be the beginning of a very sensual relationship.

TIED & EMOTIONAL

Cut a deck of cards or roll a die for who goes first. The higher scorer gets to tie their lover up, explore and tease them at their pleasure! Here's the catch: it's your partner's turn next, and they earn the right to do to you exactly what you've done to them! When you begin, keep one eye on the clock and time how long it takes for you to put your erotic imagination—and your partner's pleasure—through its paces. That's exactly how long they get to exact their "retribution" on you!

This is light-hearted fun. Only indulge in power games when you both feel, realistically, that you have enough trust between you. Agree a "safe" word that your lover's not likely to say during sex unless they really want you to stop and release them. Don't think you'll need a wardrobe full of silk ropes and leather straps—gentleness is the key and their helplessness is largely token, so a couple of sheer scarves, or other ribbons or fabrics, will do the job. Don't knot them tightly enough to restrict circulation. Make sure your lover's comfortable, and act out what you believe they'll like, not your own fantasies. Blindfold and surprise them. You'll get what you give, so be nice!

✱ *Play a competitive game—and feel your adrenaline pumping—before making love.*

✱ *Try doing everything your partner tells you for fifteen minutes.*

✱ *Discuss boundaries before trying kinky stuff. Agree a "safe" word for games to stop. This should be something non-sexual.*

✱ *Pick a word that's likely to come up in conversation, and touch or kiss your partner every time it does.*

TIPS

✱ *Relax, don't do it! In getting carried away with your own pleasure, don't forget the value of a good tease. If you back off from whatever you're doing just as your partner's about to come, they won't thank you. However, a little earlier, and you'll have them begging for more.*

✱ *If you're interested in power-play, think what words, phrases, and attitudes really do it for you both.*

✱ *Have a tickling match.*

INDEX